Hitchhiking the Highway of Tears

Hitchhiking the Highway of Tears

Poems

Sheila Nickerson

MoonPathPress

Copyright © 2017 Sheila Nickerson

All rights reserved. No part of this publication may be reproduced distributed or transmitted in any form or by any means whatsoever without written permission from the publisher, except in the case of brief excerpts for critical reviews and articles. All inquiries should be addressed to MoonPath Press.

Poetry

ISBN 978-1-936657-31-5

Cover photo: Courtesy of Mike Criss

Author photo: Courtesy of Kalie Presteen

Design: Tonya Namura using Gentium Basic

MoonPath Press is dedicated to publishing the finest poets of the U.S. Pacific Northwest.

MoonPath Press

PO Box 445

Tillamook, OR 97141

MoonPathPress@gmail.com

http://MoonPathPress.com

For Martin and all who travel with me

Table of Contents

PART I: *Along the Alaska Highway*

5   Along the Alaska Highway
6   From the East: First Light, Gastineau Channel
7   In the Compass of Unrest
8   #34, Songs of the Pine-Wife
9   Juneau Fairy Tale
10   Palm Sunday: Friends Church, Kotzebue
11   The Village Teacher
12   Wild Swans at Mid-Winter
13   To Tom, at Ten, Who Catches Mice
14   The News from Nikolai
15   Notes from the Umiak-Maker, Kamchatka
16   A Woman Speaks: Western Alaska
17   The Muskrat Hunter Remembers
18   Notes from a Last Summer
19   The Priest Visits Toksook Bay
20   On the Alaska Ferry, along the British Columbia Coast
21   Early Morning, Late August
22   Promise, in September
23   Kodiak Widow
24   Kooshdaka Visits My Daughter
25   Skagway: The House on Main Street
26   Lynette's Story
27   Skunk Cabbage Visits Southeast Alaska
28   When Spring Came and the Blue Bear Came to Town
29   Iris
30   Visitors
31   Tiger Lilies
32   Thimbleberry
33   School Desk as Garden: Tenakee Springs

34 Tenakee Springs Garden: January
35 The Foxglove, Gone Feral: Calhoun Ave.
36 In the Stone Nursery
37 Evensong
38 Trees
39 The Dolly Varden Char: Its Name, Its Dance, Its Prize
40 In an August Garden, along the Path in Tenakee Springs
41 The Abandoned Russian Orthodox Church, Aleknagik: September
42 A Friend Writes, to Say She Is Leaving Alaska
43 April Night When the Full Moon Is Brighter Than the Northern Lights
44 Song of the Soapstone Carver
45 Illumination
46 Pelican of the Wilderness
47 Choosing Pansies: Landscape Alaska
48 Neighbor
49 Wishkita: House of the Shark
50 On Reading a Recipe for Pickled Venison Heart
52 White Lilacs
53 Juneau: On the Accidental Visit of a Northern Pygmy Owl
54 With Jean, Picking Blueberries in the Juneau Woods
55 How I Know Another Summer Has Ended
56 In the Raspberry Villages: September
57 Summer Ends in the High Latitudes

PART II: *Hitchhiking the Highway of Tears*
61 Traveling Highway 16, British Columbia
62 Russ, in the Dark Garden
63 The Eagle's Nest

64 After Euthanasia: Kern National Wildlife Refuge
65 Detour: Driving North on I-5
66 Summer, by Bicycle
67 Traveling East, from the Oregon Coast
68 In the Gardens at Padden Creek
69 Sailing in the San Juan Islands: Late August
70 In a University Town: September
71 October Hollyhocks
72 With an Old Dog in the Autumn Woods
73 December Dusk: The Stables off Smith Road
74 Tapping the Sugar Maple Trees: Millbrook
75 At Virginia Mason Hospital: March
76 June: On the West Flank of Mt. Baker
77 Transplanting the Poppies
78 The Summer of Dead Birds
79 At Summer's End
80 During the Moon of Falling Leaves
81 September: Collecting the Plums
82 At Hannah's Wedding: September, Cama Beach State Park
83 The Gardener, in October
84 The Loneliness of the Late Afternoon Cook
85 Charlie and His Water Lily
86 The Almost Abandoned House, Old Route 213, High Falls
87 The Walkers, Ulster County
88 Winter on the Banks of the Delaware and Hudson Canal
89 Late Winter in High Falls: Waiting for the School Bus
90 The Apple Trees, Rolling Downhill to the Banks of Padden Creek
91 The Lost Gospel of the Cooper's Hawk
92 In the Kitchen
93 Tortellini Arrives at the Front Steps

94 With Splendora, My Friend, among the Tomatoes
95 On Approaching a Fiftieth Wedding Anniversary
96 On the Origin of Stories

99 Acknowledgments
109 About the Author

Hitchhiking the Highway of Tears

PART I
Along the Alaska Highway

Along the Alaska Highway

The night the pigs disappeared from
Johnny Friend's corral at Watson Lake
there were no answers. What could climb
a fence as high as that and be so neat?
In all these years we have not learned.
More mysteries have crowded in,
deaths and other silences that make us think
of what must fill the space between the stars.
Now, in the second quadrant,
in the year of solar storms,
night sky burns. You tell me how,
when you camped at Watson Lake,
you might have heard Sasquatch.
The map of years says little—
a red line bending north,
you there, me here. These names—
Swift River, Jakes Corner, Destruction Bay—
are only places. The true coordinates
are locked in blood. Tell me again the sound
you heard, tell me again the height
of Johnny Friend's corral at Watson Lake.

From the East: First Light, Gastineau Channel

Imagine moving like that, over each mountain,
touching each tree, leaf, needle.
Imagine my fingers, tracing your face,
illuminating the map of all those years—
even the ones before I first set out,
brave and full of love, into that strange land.

In the Compass of Unrest

Radioactivity lives in the lichen,
burns in the bones of caribou.
Magnetism wavers.
In the compass of unrest
we wander, unable to find
the point of true beginning.
There was a bad shaman
claiming that he traveled to the moon.
Voices rose from the frozen ground.
Spirits lured us out to sea.
We have exchanged stories,
Danced to drums and masks,
held each other.
Now it is time to go.
The cold is nothing, the loss,
because of what we knew—
that longing which calls us
as the winds of grass call caribou.

#34, Songs of the Pine-Wife

Sharks catch in the gill nets at Skagway.
Ships founder in Peril Strait.
The pilot—the one who loved my friend—
flies out of the sky, somewhere.
Dredging the dark we find
only the depth of mystery.
Sonar and radar halt.
Locator beacons are mute.
The miles of possibility
grow inward: the final forest
where we hesitate,
children at a doorless house.

Juneau Fairy Tale

You wake one morning
with a swan's wing for an arm.
Lopsided, you move to the window;
there is wind and rain over the marsh.
Autumn flocks are flying.
You stretch, unevenly.
Your children, your mate recoil,
their words a gabble around you.
You have no taste for food,
nor can you hold a fork.
Plates, newspapers slip to the floor.
You open the door, reading weather,
trying to remember: just how you reach,
how you find your way into the air.

Palm Sunday: Friends Church, Kotzebue

First, there is the sky, an eternity. Then there is the cold, bright as a blue torch. Next comes the only bell in Kotzebue, rigged up in a frame tower on the snow, like a drill. Then, the dark entry way, a tunnel between lights, leads into the vestibule. Toilet paper on a hanger is attached to a bookcase of hymnals to borrow. An Eskimo couple with baby are there to help. Inside, flowered parkas rise like gardens, hybrid, in two languages. An old woman asks for forgiveness of Jesus and her friends. She weeps because they spat in Jesus' face. She wipes away the tears and asks to sing the hymn, "His Eye Is on the Sparrow," and the congregation does. Then one by one they state their grief. There are no sparrows yet in Kotzebue, only snowbirds and the crows. Caribou hang frozen from second-story windows. One week later, the night of Easter Eve, Charlie Rich, Jack's hunting partner, battled evil spirits out on Kobuk Lake. They tried to make him leave the trail with his dogs and turn the sled towards Noorvik, but he won.

The Village Teacher

I went to Aleknagik that winter,
read 103 books.
From the top of their houses,
the sled dogs barked at me.
I never learned the language
of the grass talking along the road.

I waited for spring—
a prince dressed in bells—
to find me, saying,
I will lead you away
from this tiny place.
I will give you the colors of dawn.
I will spread them out
for your bed. You will
never again need words.

He would show me the way across the lake
to the nest of the emperor geese—
or even past the mountains of the Kuskokwim—
and I would be his silent bride
bought for a clutch of leaves.

Wild Swans at Mid-Winter

Last night wild swans flew into my heart.
It happened while I was writing a letter
to someone I love who is far away.
One of the Chinese poets would have known
how to put it: the stirring, the cry,
the darkness settling down,
the lamplight falling on my empty hand.

To Tom, at Ten, Who Catches Mice

Down in the basement you take charge.
You bait the traps, you place the traps,
you wait until they're full. Your bounty,
$1.00 per. The price keeps going up.
You are taller, Tom, the mice smaller,
their ears round and soft as leaves.
This time, they've gotten into the jelly,
last summer's blueberries gone.
You will avenge, you will set right
down in that dark world of wax and jam,
each time, Tom, the mice smaller in your hand.

The News from Nikolai

The news comes late from Nikolai:
a fire there has claimed three lives.
The land around is still.
Christmas has not come.
Between Farewell and Poorman
seasons come in ragged clothes,
the beggar summer quietest of all.

Notes from the Umiak-Maker, Kamchatka

In churches, Sergei said,
bell ropes are made
from baby walrus skin
and umiaks, the open boats,
are made only from
female walrus skin split
and oiled with whale oil.
An umiak can be a drum
as well as hunting vessel.
Listen to it now, beating
out its call as church bells
ring, the sea filling with cries.

A Woman Speaks: Western Alaska

It takes the kindness of strangers.
In the fall, we collect the Eskimo potato,
masru, from the burrows of mice,
reaching carefully into their holes.
We leave a piece of dried fish in exchange,
but let the mice do the work for us.
When wind blows and snow covers the tundra,
we remember: the banks of the river
where we hunted, the tiny paths swept away.

The Muskrat Hunter Remembers

Long ago, when we hunted muskrat by canoe,
the grasses opened before us.
One lake became another.
Now, if I paddled all the way to Old Minto,
I could not tell the news:
how the birch bark rotted,
how the lake became empty,
how the bones of the boat
finally gave up, too,
and lay down to rest
where the muskrats rest.

Notes from a Last Summer
(Addendum to the journal of Lieutenant George W. De Long, Commander of the Jeannette, fatally caught in the polar ice, 1879-1881)

When the Chinese cooks flew kites,
running parallel with the ship,
we stopped our chores and watched:
birds and insects—sudden summer
where summer cannot be.
Ah Sam and Charles Tong Sing,
you hunted bears, too.
But you gave us kites—
better than rainbows and Ross's gulls,
better even than Newcomb's mosquitoes.
You led us back to dreams of grass.
Your scraps of color freed us,
cutting paths through frozen hope
back to the gardens of home and
afternoons of strawberries and cream.

The Priest Visits Toksook Bay

Here, the lamb of God
is a little reindeer.
And there is no sacrifice,
only survival.
The words of the mystery
fly like the snow,
to no one certain place.
But language for mercy
is tracks to the village beyond
over still waters, frozen.

On the Alaska Ferry, along the British Columbia Coast

Sailing past Cape Caution,
I think of the lighthouse keeper's daughter,
how she waits each week for helicopter drops—
those pieces of mail carefully aimed at her door.
Her view is of Queen Charlotte Sound,
where swells carry us rolling north.
And what if I sent her, somehow,
a pair of shoes encrusted with jewels
to dance on her rocky shore?
The dance of the lighthouse keeper's daughter
would amaze blue mussels and clams.
Rubies and emeralds would fall to the sand,
seed pearls shine in the moon.
The tide would return as usual,
and everything would go on as before.
But the lighthouse keeper's daughter,
her heart now ignited by beauty,
would know the source of light—
the fire inside the reefs her father
gave as yard, as fence, as school.

Early Morning, Late August

Jo had just arrived from Fairbanks,
by ferry, on her way to California.
It was Friday morning. I was walking the dog,
reviewing distance, how we travel, disappear.
Suddenly, a rainbow, out of amber clouds;
then, across the rainbow,
a wedge of ducks, flying south.
I knew winter to be a curtain,
distance an illusion.
But if I had gone a minute later,
I would have missed all that;
I would not have called Jo outside.
We would not have been two friends
standing in the middle of the street
beside her car with the moose rack tied
on top both pointing and exclaiming at the sky.

Promise, in September

Finally, only nasturtiums are left.
But we will go, Beth, to the wetlands in May
to watch for the black-crowned night herons
which visited last spring.
We will see what comes through
these blank winter walls: the divide.
A few letters will make it,
a visitor or two with tales
of elephants and dancing bears—
perhaps word of a friend;
then, in April, Sandhill cranes and hummingbirds.
We will take the trail from the airport
out through the tall wet grass.
Waiting, we will know at dusk
if what we hope is true.
And if it's not, we will have seen
the tide flats on an evening in late spring
with the plumage of the wind
spread across the sky;
we will have come through, after all.

Kodiak Widow

The curtains speak to me.
Even the spoons
slipping in and out of my mouth
don't know as much—
the man who seeded me,
the sons who swam away
like fingerlings.
The curtains tell me how it was—
how I unfurled like sails before wind,
how I shook with light,
danced with storm.
Now when gales blow
south from the Barren Islands,
the curtains sing to me—
sometimes a lullaby in Russian,
sometimes a song
that only I can understand.
I need no instrument, no telephone.
The curtains hold the news,
the gossip of flying geese and tears.

Kooshdaka Visits My Daughter

Kooshdaka, spirit of land otter,
walks the alley behind my house.
Helen saw him, one Fourth of July night,
aroused from the creek by sluice racers.
He stood, looking at her in late twilight;
he was almost as tall as she.
He turned and disappeared, as since
the bear and porcupine have disappeared
into the unaccountable woods,
and Helen has grown away into her own world.
In the villages, on the edge of the ocean,
people avoid talking about Kooshdaka—how he steals souls,
takes them right out of a human who is left,
then, scrambling for clams on the beach,
his teeth and nails wrecked by digging, by biting.
Sometimes such a person is found, staring emptily
to sea. Kooshdaka explains certain disappearances.
Now Kooshdaka glides past garbage cans in my alley
while I lie in bed turning the pages of the dark,
searching the beaches of sleep for the faces that are lost.

Skagway: The House on Main Street

Close by the city dump
where wild pigs make their home,
this house, by winter twilight:
a line of tiny onyx pigs,
pink on a window ledge
looking east with candles
never lit; and in the
large backyard, bikes and
Christmases of broken toys.
Once a woman entered here
with hope. Still she speaks
to plants, but only when
there is no one to hear.
This she now knows: Her
children can grow without
her; the pot she stirs is
no stew of gypsy tears;
one day these pigs will
no longer rim her window
catching dawn and dusk.
Her name (that might be
Grace, or Emily) will be
cast in stone under snow,
under droves of rooting light.

Lynette's Story

The summer the common loon did not return,
I watched from the window.
And the foxgloves, too, climbing their stairway
of blossoms, did not come back.
My father died, my brother unreconciled.
At the burial, a monarch butterfly
flew from the flower arrangements,
and as suddenly was gone.
My house is on the beach.
A whale's sounding can fill much space,
harebells on the rocks, and catnip growing
by the backdoor for the desire of Sadie.
I go inland now to clean my father's house,
to shut each drawer forever.
I will take only his eyes;
they know where loons and foxgloves go,
a son lost, a daughter gardening by the sea.

Skunk Cabbage Visits Southeast Alaska

In the green revival tent
at the edge of the woods,
spring speaks in yellow tongues,
fleshly and foul smelling.
Many do not heed the call.
She must return, each year,
setting up in swampy meadows—
even in ditches along the road—
and every time, the tent fills,
and we make promises again.

When Spring Came and the Blue Bear Came to Town

When the blue bear came to town,
we played our saxophone.
Listening, it shook its head in salmonberry bushes,
pushed and rooted in the earth.
It came each night, at dusk,
to Gastineau—the avenue at the edge—
to our Dumpsters, porches, and steps
sagging with rain.
We played, we sang, we clapped our hands,
hoping it would cross to us;
but it came only as far as our garbage,
then turned back. We, too, returned home,
speaking of the wildness of it,
the blueness of it—like glaciers, like denim.
We could not find the words.
We followed, each night, as far as we dared,
with our saxophone, with our French horn—
a line of minstrels bound to a cave
through a wood of ancient spruce
wild as cellos not yet carved.

Iris

To pick it brings rain.
To explain its anatomy
is to be lost
in the wild flags of your eyes.
To stand beside it
in the rain-bringing meadows
calling your name is to know
June's blue tongue;
to embrace, the cry of sky and grass.

Visitors

Suppose that those tiger lilies—
there by the open door—
knocked and were admitted,
their freckled faces
orange with embarrassment.
They could not keep
from tracking dirt across
the floor, but then, that door
is held wide open by a shovel,
as if someone who loves earth
had gone inside to rest.

Tiger Lilies

That winter,
we slept like tiger lilies.
There, in our bulbs,
we listened to stories of earth,
just as the bear in its den
listens to all we say
(and that is why we must not say its name).
And when we woke, covered with color,
the bear was gone and the mammoth.
No matter how we tried—
how wide we opened our mouths to ask—
we could not learn why.

Thimbleberry

It opens five white pages
to the weather,
bright tongue at its center.
It repeats itself
mile after mile
down the midsummer road
till any passerby
must know it by heart.
It never says,
next are berries,
a wild communion,
and afterwards comes winter.
And the woods, standing pew
after pew behind it,
say nothing,
as if they could not speak.

School Desk as Garden: Tenakee Springs

The child's wildest dream:
the desk, its top torn off,
sent outside to stand forever
with dirt in its mouth—
told to make flowers.

Tenakee Springs Garden: January

The rusted wheelchair
left outside holds
only pans of rain.
Around it, broken crab
legs cover beds
till strawberries
can rise and walk again.

The Foxglove, Gone Feral: Calhoun Ave.

Imagine standing like that
on the hillside—a tribe—
each stalk close
but rooted apart.
Imagine: late summer,
top heavy with last
blossoms bending
this way and that,
as if to reach out
and touch goodbye.

In the Stone Nursery

When stone gives birth to her child,
birds stir in their nests.
Otherwise it is quiet, night.
In the morning, gardeners
rarely note the bright new stone.
Already it has learned to hide;
it has learned to be perfectly still.

Evensong

The little brown bat at the forest's edge
hangs on the wing of evening.
Trees swell with their stories.
The moment of the trail opens,
and we pass through easily,
whispering leaf, needle, sap.
As the heron flies to its nest,
we grow tall and slow
with the voices of moss.
Good night is all we can recall.
Goodnight.   Goodnight.   Goodnight.

Trees

"What are they thinking, the sheep on the hills?"
—Bryan Guinness

What are they thinking, the trees on the hills?
They could be the souls of those who fell
on their way to heaven or those who loved
this place too much and decided to root
in the rocks instead of ascending in light.
They are transformed in snow; they could be
an order of angels sent by Oertha, guard
of the north. They carry layers of light and
dark in their arms; they could be records of
time, played over by needles of wind and ice,
or messengers waiting for orders to run
down the slopes with their sharp, green words.
What are they doing, the trees on the hills—
remembering fogs and springtimes of fern?
Before we grow old, we must go to them there
on the slopes and ask them how it will be
when we climb into other shapes—and if theirs
is a good one to take, holding green to the hills.

The Dolly Varden Char: Its Name, Its Dance, Its Prize

It is said we are named
for a dress print, a flower-sprinkled
dimity worn by a coquette in Dickens.
But fiction and clothes came later.
We danced at the first ball of the river,
winning the prize for beauty:
the right to swim from lake to sea.
Every stripe, spot, and pattern was there,
in colors not found above, and we won.
Ever since, the other side of water
has been attempting imitations. See
how their fashions change, their flowers fade.
Even their novelists fall short.

In an August Garden, along the Path in Tenakee Springs

A plaster angel, small and blue,
broods on an ornamental bridge
over an infant creek.
Next to it—that could be God's house:
peeling white paint, lace curtains,
china figurines on windowsills.
God could be inside, sculpting,
while listening to records
large and slow as spiders' work.
But it is only an old one
who hobbles out at dusk
to stand beside delphiniums
on the incoherent bank
waiting for the creek's first words.

The Abandoned Russian Orthodox Church, Aleknagik: September

Sometimes villages must get up and go.
Sometimes a congregation moves,
leaving no one behind but those
who cannot carry their crosses.
We will never know where they went
or how we might recognize them.
Sitting on the steps of the empty church,
we know only this: fireweed does not care.
It talks with the wind as if no one
were listening, as if we did not exist—
strangers who soon would be gone,
leaving nothing behind.

A Friend Writes, to Say She Is Leaving Alaska

You are moving, you say, to Magadan.
Already fireweed is fading at its peak,
and autumn whispers in the stalks.
It isn't far—across the Bering Strait,
down to the sea of Okhotsk.
There, they will write your name
in a different alphabet
and call to you with different sounds.
Because of what has happened,
all inexplicable, we might not meet again.
You have sent me a dried columbine
and a business card in Russian.
Long ago, explorers set out on such a trip,
knowing less than you and I.
They looked for birds and read the sky.
We can do no less.
There, inside this envelope of stars—
a letter bright as sparrows,
a map of bluest lupine
written on a hillside far away.

April Night When the Full Moon Is Brighter Than the Northern Lights

A small button moon moves up the sky
searching for a hole,
but seamless night does not oblige.
What is lost and mismatched must travel loose.
See, Mother Wind opens her button box
and we tumble out, rolling across the dark:
some shining, some not, all made of bone.

Song of the Soapstone Carver

In my hand, the stone:
already it knows its shape
and lives—an animal or bird—
already with its wings or feet
set on certain flight.

Follow, fingers, the slow terrain
of dreams within a rock.
Cut away the dark forgetting,
a geology of loss.

Come, ptarmigan or fox released,
and know the loving knife.

Illumination

Sometimes, when evening light
is like sea water
and daffodils sit in every chair,
I see the shape we will become.
Lacking angles, it is without pain.
Lacking words, it is precise.
Lacking skin, it is equal.
It is the surrender of walls
at the moment
when crab apples blossom in fog.

Pelican of the Wilderness

I am lying on my waterbed
In Juneau, Alaska,
reading how Jean Harris killed Dr. Tarnower
In Scarsdale, New York.
Sam flips on the TV.
Billy Graham appears, exhorting:
"I am like a pelican of the wilderness.
I am like an owl of the desert."
Sam switches channels.
Billy Graham goes away,
replaced by a plane crash in California.
I continue reading my book,
then remember the black bear
bounding out of the blackness
only last Saturday as we drove
Tait home; and know, in that opening
between dinner and eternity,
the level of wonder at which we live:
a bear caught in the headlights, dazed;
we breaking out of the moment's womb,
amazed, into each new wilderness of soul.

Choosing Pansies: Landscape Alaska

I stand with Dave, the nurseryman,
In his fief of yellow pansies.
We discuss Tom, my son, his friend,
now climbing Mt. St. Elias to the north.
Wind blows from an uncertain direction.
I ask if the hanging baskets
can withstand the cold.
Dave says yes, and I say yes,
let pansies and violas bloom
sunny and blue in this sharp rain
which blossoms into snow for Tom.

Neighbor

Suppose that old woman—
I have seen her once—
living in that small green house
is related to raspberries.
They alone climb up her walk
every spring and reach till
they can peek in the windows.
I have seen no one—
not even dog or pigeon—
go up that path
in any season. And suppose
that she dies in winter
and that is why her path
is never cleared of snow
and that she rises in spring
with red sap, a vision,
to be met at the door
by her cousins coming for summer.
They carry bags packed tight,
they gossip like mad.
Leaning against each other,
they dress up,
they whisper of red,
they dream of sleep that follows fruit.
And suppose that we
opened her door in winter
and found her there,
A tiny nest of roots.

Wishkita: House of the Shark

In the Indian Village
houses lean.
There I saw my friend,
her child, her lover.
She had come on the ferry
from Sitka to be with him.
Later, she left her husband,
her child, her Tlingit lover.
The burnt roof of Wishkita
opens further to sky,
unsleeping as the eye of shark
for which it is named.
Every day, passing by,
I remember her like that:
open to a fierce light.

On Reading a Recipe for Pickled Venison Heart
after Tom Has Left for School

Soak heart two hours in salt water.
Clean out all blood. Drain.
Boil with poppy seeds, garlic, thyme,
and bay leaf till tender. Refrigerate two days.
Cover with chianti. Refrigerate one week.
Slice thinly, serve with horseradish
and Jewish pumpernickel.

I remember the head of the buck,
velvet antlers, dark eyes staring
into the basement wall,
and the haunches hanging from the beams.
His face did not feel cold.

You were nineteen when you shot him
on Mt. Jumbo—the summer you also
met the bears. The younger boys
helped carry the pieces down.
You left the heart on the mountain
as any hunter would.

We ate venison for a birthday feast.
Then, next day, you left,
flying out of the forest.
You call, we talk. Yes,
we continue to eat venison.

Winter comes, with rain.
You shot the buck through one lung,
piercing the spine.
It died instantly.
I add onions, carrots.

The heart has flown with crows
over the hemlock green.
It will never soak in salt
nor float in wine.

It will know only what the forest knows.
Next summer, Tom, when you come back,
we will all be closer to the forest's heart.

White Lilacs

The bitter widow
who lives down the street
grows white lilacs,
or, white lilacs
have taken hold
beside her door.
I want her to open
that door with a shout,
rush down the steps,
embrace those lilacs like friends
long gone on a journey,
hug them and cry
and dance in the yard
and sing to the neighbors
that everything beautiful
comes again and again,
claiming no one can be lonely
who does not choose to be;
and then we will all dance
until the lilacs burst
into summer, and only
when tired will we stop
to rest in a quiet place
called winter.

Juneau: On the Accidental Visit of a Northern Pygmy Owl

Pygmy owl of my heart,
blown by a storm
to the south wall of our house:
I want everyone to be safe.
Is there a hospital near?
How many beats are left
inside our brittle ribs?
When the wind lifts
and you are gone,
I will hold you warm
in my pocket:
small as a sparrow,
large as the world I hunt.

With Jean, Picking Blueberries in the Juneau Woods

As we pick, we discuss journals—
the Tolstoys and their agony,
L. M. Montgomery and her passion
barely contained by the tales
of her Prince Edward Island home.
It is good to be here together,
friends collecting the work
of the northern woods
as day rolls into the pail of night.
All around us, another crop—
stories bursting to be told—
stretches as far as the trees,
a feast, but we must go.
The library of leaves has closed
and we have chosen what to take.

How I Know Another Summer Has Ended

The Sandhill cranes have reached Gustavus,
staging on their way south.
I would send you letters
folded in their wings
and stamped with bits of sky—
not to read but to hear:
page after page
delivering news I cannot write.

In the Raspberry Villages: September

In the raspberry villages
strung out along the alleys,
the news is mostly bad.
There is rumor of storms from the north,
more disappearances.
Even the birds, those summer enemies,
have fled, and all who come to pick.
Neighbors watch each other fall
but are helpless.
Yet, out of the ground comes a hum like a river,
word of a warm red cave in the place of roots
where strength is building. Some even say,
Now, let us go. It is time to enter the earth.

Summer Ends in the High Latitudes

and the Red Cross asks for blood.
The light is empty now,
drained of birds and flowers,
sharp as glass.
At night, porcupines dressed
in stegosaurus silhouettes
patrol our sidewalks
seeking last raspberry canes.
We need Type O, the Red Cross says:
the universal type, my type.
But I cannot give my blood away,
not now with light so clear,
not now with branches taut
in the waiting room of cold.

PART II
Hitchhiking the Highway of Tears

Traveling Highway 16, British Columbia

Along Highway 16, between the ocean and the Coast Mountains,
women disappear, some into black trucks,
some into black space.
Now it's called the "Highway of Tears,"
with billboards warning women not to hitchhike,
but they do—to get to work.
There are more missing-person cases now than towns,
and the god of lost cartography needs to make
a new map, replacing Prince Rupert, Terrace, Smithers,
and Burns Lake with Ramona, Roxanne, Lana, Tamara.
We must find Nicole along the rushing Skeena
and travel from Alisha to Delphine and on to Gloria
to find the abandoned hamlet of Maddy, once loud
but now a silent grove. We must search the black lakes
and follow black bears and ask the old, black trees
where these lovely spirits fled, and where,
as they resettled, they shed their bones and shoes.

Russ, in the Dark Garden

It is convenient to have a neighbor
who is an astronomer. You can ask
him what it is you see in the sky,
not having to bother with books or almanacs.
He tells you how the mother raccoon
washes her babies, one by one,
in the bird bath at four in the morning.
You can sleep till dawn because
he is watching for you. Also, he keeps
track of the spirits in our adjoining
gardens, a way station, he says,
but you don't have to worry
about the afterlife because he is there
as a traffic cop, a kind one, telling
the displaced to move on. You can sleep.
Is it Mars or Jupiter?
Is it Harry, our deceased friend, who keeps
making strange things happen,
like breaking the glass at the party?
Russ will explain and take care of it.
You can sleep, and when you wake and go out,
everything will look as it always has: at rest.

The Eagle's Nest

Sometimes cats come to visit
in this dark and dangerous universe.
After a storm, Beth found an eagle's nest
blown down in her yard in Blaine—
and in it, twenty cat collars.
What to do?
Where there were numbers, she called,
but most, on hearing her question,
did not want to hear the answer.
They did not want to hear,
as if the cats could still be there,
sitting just outside the door,
waiting to be called.

After Euthanasia: Kern National Wildlife Refuge

At the vet's, they call it
"the time to say goodbye,"
which sounds so much better
than "putting to sleep"
or, "putting down," when
what they really mean
is "stopping the heart."
Holding you, I felt yours stop,
strong and even to the last beat.
Afterwards, Copper, we drove
the Pacific Flyway south,
following the snow geese
all the way to Lost Hills
but did not find you. Instead,
there in the wildlife refuge,
a barn owl with its pale
heart-shaped face rose
from a tree in front of us,
circling in hunt, and a coyote
jumped from a ditch beside us.
Can anyone explain this—
an owl in sunlight,
a sudden coyote,
a heart I caused to stop?

Detour: Driving North on I-5

One March day you come upon a town
called, perhaps, Canyon Creek, deep
in Oregon's woods. You pass a house,
plain and white, white curtains
at the windows, white cat smiling in the yard,
small white daisies spreading through the lawn.
Along the path leading to the porch, iris leaves
jut up, sharp and bare. Suddenly you know
this is where Iris, messenger of gods, has gone;
and when she leaves, everywhere she steps
will bloom, this house and yard fusing
into rainbows. *She's here!* You want to knock
upon the door and shout, to catch her and confront her
in her golden wings and ask—oh so many things—
but do not dare, for Spring is not the only news she bears;
and you have much that waits behind your own front door.

Summer, by Bicycle

Summer comes by bicycle.
I know this because, in early June,
a bike was left resting against
a Douglas fir at the trail head
and stayed there, unlocked,
until late in August.
No one knows where it came from
or exactly when it left. No one
knows what summer does all day,
ambling about in the woods,
fumbling in shaggy pockets,
sometimes forgetting
and leaving things behind.

Traveling East, from the Oregon Coast

Along the dark road, miles from Elsie,
a table with flowers for sale:
though no one attends but the trees
locked in their giant gloom,
I know the girl who placed them there.
Drying her hands, she then sets off for school,
pretending to be like the others.
Careful to wear bright colors,
she carries no mud on her shoes,
makes sure her fingernails are clean.
But all day in the airless room
she stretches out,
riding whispers of fir,
till she can touch the house
the forest built for her, their golden bride.
Satisfied, she carries out those acts
the handless trees cannot.
Sometimes they ask, Go—
Pick dahlias. Place them by the road.
Sometimes, they say (in voices low as moss),
Stroke me, stroke me, and she does,
a clutch of petals waving as we pass.

In the Gardens at Padden Creek

Standing in the nursery she owns,
Mary tells me of the kestrel she kept
in her childhood room in New Mexico,
how it was followed by a raven,
and of the horse she rode to school.
Last month when Mary's long-haired cat—
Emily of the Flowers—died, I grieved.
Last night, one of Mary's Polish
Spirit hens was killed by a raccoon.
Her mate scratches in the Sunday shade
of cottonwoods silvering, apples reddening.
I buy lavender, pink zinnias, and think
I still can fill the empty spaces,
I still can dig and make color grow.

Sailing in the San Juan Islands: Late August

The park ranger at Suchia Island
hangs his wash between grapes
and sunflowers. Leaving the boat,
I approach his gate guarded by a
Blue Heeler and picture him inside
his cabin, writing. Our passage
was rough, nights now cold.
Soon his garden must be turned
and color stripped from Rosario Strait.
His solar panels will stay open,
but sky will slide shut,
along with every cockpit on the coast.
No letters will make it out; and I
will stop remembering—his laundry,
his dog, his chimney, its smoke.

In a University Town: September

The hills blacken with berries.
Then comes that other harvest—
couches found along streets and alleys.
On sidewalks, porches, and lawns
they spring up, "for free," often
brown, puckered, and soft,
as if left too long to ripen.
Dented with stories, they wait
to be taken away, but sometimes
rain comes first; and then what?
I have seen people attack them
with axes as if to undo
the history that shaped them so,
but they grow right back,
bursting with truth,
the fruit we leave by the road.

October Hollyhocks

Across the street, hollyhocks reach
to the eaves, even pushing at the peak.
My neighbors, away at work,
are unaware of these attempts
to penetrate their house.
When they return, near dark,
other things are on their minds.
Tragedy is everywhere, knocking
hard on hearts and doors across America.
I cannot blame them, these neighbors
with remote controls, operating their
garage and driving in to disappear
before flowers have a chance to speak.

With an Old Dog in the Autumn Woods

An old dog listens more carefully
than a young dog
to sounds in the autumn woods.
See—the old one, head cocked
to the falling of leaves,
while the young one romps.

Yes, Copper, you and I hear
noises we cannot name:
footsteps in the wind.
Come close and we will watch
the young one as he runs.

December Dusk: The Stables off Smith Road

Behind me, in the arena, horses play.
In front, across the field, coyotes yip and howl.
The dogs run out, barking.
I call them back, call and call.
Finally the small ones come,
but the large one stays, holding his ground.
And who would dare to cross, either way,
where barking melds with howling,
stubble stiffens with cold,
and a winter night steps out of the woods?

Tapping the Sugar Maple Trees: Millbrook
For Zeb

Just before dark,
we go to the secret buckets,
take out the frozen blood,
which looks and tastes like water.
You boil it all night,
all morning, till it turns
thick and gold, a gift.

Breaking through the crusted snow,
through quiet bittersweet,
I know we could be like that:
enchanted trees needing only
taps, needing only fire,
and someone who believes.

At Virginia Mason Hospital: March

Inside the emergency entrance,
a man holds a box of tulips, open and red.
In Holland, during the war, people
ate tulip bulbs to stay alive
until the swastika faded.
Now, in this camp of accident and pain,
the box begins to move through halls,
and we who watch fall back and bow
before the chalice of spring's blood.

June: On the West Flank of Mt. Baker

The cougars are back:
first two sheep gone, then the calf,
while that careless shepherd Summer
wanders about in the fields,
scattering color as if there were no end.
Why do we invite him back each year,
knowing he will break our hearts,
knowing he will leave when he chooses,
taking away all that he has touched?

Transplanting the Poppies

Savior has given me plants
taken from his old house.
His wife has died and he is moving.
Poppies can go, too. Marie would
like that: roots being driven across town
as if to a party. Marie would wear
a red dress and her lovely smile.
"Now Daddy," she would say to Savior,
"Be careful." If only we could
forget that Marie now lives
in a small box by Savior's bed,
we would tell her how glad we are
to be traveling on together
across town and time
to find an untried soil
where we can bloom again.

The Summer of Dead Birds

The summer we folded those six fallen
birds into the garden—ruby-crowned
kinglet, starlings, fledgling,
pink-footed pigeon—the yellowing
came early. I knew how it would be:
the fluttering, with a thousand
leaves in spasm and night hurtling
at us. We had hit a wall of glass
or caught our foot in a crack;
we had plunged, winter quick on our
backs. Then the sharp-shinned hawk
struck—fastest and most beautiful of all.

At Summer's End

At summer's end
foxglove pack up
from the lowest floor.
Finally, the only blossoms
left are those at the very top:
beautiful women in an attic of wind
leaning dangerously out
for rescues that cannot be.

During the Moon of Falling Leaves

Christa took me to Mount Baker
to hunt the golden chanterelles,
but what we found instead
was little libraries of rain, freely given,
with stories spilling out from every door—
stories of shamans and of shipwrecks,
of circuses and wars.
With every door we opened,
we helped ourselves but also left
some mysteries and romances of our own,
freely given, for those who follow
after, searching through the woods.

September: Collecting the Plums

Then it was time to shake the tree,
purple plums falling to the blue
tarp spread beneath wide branches.
We filled bucket after bucket.
That night, across town at Marcia's,
while we ate and drank on the dark deck,
something cried at the edge of the woods
and a strange light crossed the sky.
Plum season stretches deep beyond trees
when the heart, too, drops what it cannot hold.

At Hannah's Wedding: September, Cama Beach State Park

In the open space between beach and woods
there were no reserved seats.
God could sit anywhere, and so could we:
a thoroughly democratic ceremony
with Saratoga Passage as a backdrop—
water, waves, and gulls all free;
and the sun sat down beside us,
an overweight uncle following us
out after the words were said,
then wandering off among the other guests.
I will remember, Hannah, the letters
from family and friends read
aloud instead of Epistles and
stories told instead of Gospels,
and how the sea with all its tongues
rolled in to say, "It's done. It's done."

The Gardener, in October

Now come juncos, those black-
hooded monks, sweeping seeds
from the aisles and pews.
You thought you understood, but
now, observing these contemplatives
among stalks that once were foxgloves,
you see: You are allowed to kneel
here, serving with your hands busy
in the earth, a novice under watch.

The Loneliness of the Late Afternoon Cook

All up and down this rainy coast,
where many houses are for rent,
dinners are being cooked in silence.
Even the stainless steel pots,
when placed upon red heat,
don't speak,
and water holds its tongue.
So many questions.
Are love and gratitude enough?
I would ask my neighbor,
but she has moved—I don't know
where—and deer have taken back
the land, a wilderness of weeds
grown up between us, a place where
animals come out to meet at night.

Charlie and His Water Lily

Today, driving to Pittsburgh in January cold,
I remember Charlie's story of water lilies.
Each spring, Charlie buys a new one for his pond.
But last year, the nurseryman said No,
it was a waste. Since Charlie commuted too
early and late, he would sell him
only a night-blooming species.
From then on, Charlie could see his young lily
only by flashlight, a marauder in his own mud.
Charlie, growing old, will soon return for another.
Of course, he could go to a different nursery;
but who else would care enough to argue with him,
to acknowledge out loud how he mounts the train
only when his lily, exhausted, folds herself in sleep?

The Almost Abandoned House, Old Route 213, High Falls

Spirits often inhabit stairs.
Look there, where sun whittled
away today at crusted snow
on the east edge of those front
steps, as if clearing a narrow
path for a small being who might
climb to the top, knock,
and ask the impossible.
Here, in this lockup of deep cold
where every passerby is suspect,
doors are blocked from the inside
by folded towel, sleeping dog,
or betrayals twisted thick like
rope against the uninvited guest.

The Walkers, Ulster County

Every town has one, at least.
In High Falls, the old woman
with stick who shuffles along
the roads. In Stone Ridge,
the young man with beard
who never slows, seldom stops.
Upsetting dogs, relentless,
they wear out curiosity
until, even though you pick
them up occasionally, you
never ask: Who was your
greatest love? Tell me
what beauty split your sky
and sent you wandering,
small planet from its star.

Winter on the Banks of the Delaware and Hudson Canal

Here on the edge of the old canal,
fire engines drank all night
from the broken pools. Still,
the Mossy Brook farm house burned
and the old man died, the one who
walked his beagle out each night
along the road, even when
their path was cut away by ice.

Late Winter in High Falls: Waiting for the School Bus

Two girls from separate houses wait
on either side of Orchard Street.
Their breath rises in the cold air,
merging with angels.
They do not speak but stand apart
in separate worlds until
the bus arrives, folds them
in, and carries them away.

Later, I learn they know each other
and I think of tulips under snow:
how, climbing from the dark,
side by side, they stretch towards sun,
bending but not touching,
until that fancy carriage,
Spring, arrives and carries them away.

The Apple Trees, Rolling Downhill to the Banks of Padden Creek

Here they come again, feral apple
trees rounded with blossoms,
rolling down hill to the creek.
At other times, they are invisible,
or perhaps in school.
Only now, in March, do we see them—
haloed white balls heedless
of black trunks
standing fruitless in their way.

The Lost Gospel of the Cooper's Hawk

Finally, there were two hens left, until that afternoon
when the Cooper's Hawk swooped down and took one.
We gave the last away; what would her life have been—
a single hen cowering beneath the sky?
Then silence stole the chicken coop.

Of course I blamed the hawk, but later
there would be different versions.
In some, the hawk would become hero;
in others, it would barely appear,
or not be properly identified,
the whole story in question.
I leave argument and theory to others—
priests on one side, witches on another.
Having had to scoop the feathers up,
I join the silence.

In the Kitchen

All day it is vespers:
forks taut in their pews,
cups hanging like bats
in the choir loft of plates.
Spoons keep their mouths
open, in case. Who can
say what makes a hymn
or heralds the opening
of doors and drawers?

Tortellini Arrives at the Front Steps

Not every tortoise who waddles up your driveway
brings a message. But sometimes you wonder.
Here is Tortellini, from Terrace Place—
a block away and down the hill—
coming toward your door. It took her four days,
her people say, and she has done this before.
Quickly, we discuss the patterns on her back,
the meaning of her visit, our dreams and fears.

But why aren't we equally amazed
each day to open up the door
and find Morning standing there
dressed in gypsy clothes?
Just think how far she's had to trudge,
what obstacles and hills to find us,
the many accidents along the way.
But there we stand, blank,
looking past her for the news
printed, wrapped in orange plastic,
tossed onto our driveway as we slept.

With Splendora, My Friend, among the Tomatoes

Summer is ending. You have cut the tomato
vines and hung them over the wall
of the empty stall where Sadie, the last horse,
lived. As you trim them, we talk, and I watch
the ghost of Sadie whose sore, foundering feet
could find no comfort. The tomatoes will ripen
here in the old barn, needing neither sun nor roots.
And when we pick them and eat them,
stories of summer will run through our blood.
Sadie will look up, testing the air. Then,
light of foot, she will canter across our thoughts,
reminding us how, when her body fell,
three doves flew overhead.

On Approaching a Fiftieth Wedding Anniversary

We had lived so many years
together we could barely remember.
Then the hummingbird flew
inside the house, beating against
the highest window. We trapped
it between two brooms and carried
it outside. After resting a moment,
it flew away, out of sight.
The house is silent now. After all
these years, there is little more
to say. This was no fairy tale,
no magic, only two people grown
old together almost holding in their
hands a free and iridescent life.

On the Origin of Stories

Suppose a peddler came to your door
to sell you the story of your life.
It was one of many he had in a bag;
but this one was yours.
You would have held it to the light,
observing it from different angles,
shrugged before buying.
Often you have thought of the peddler
but have settled in with what you got.
He picked it specially for you.
Sometimes it stirs on the shelf where you put it,
but you ignore it. The door has opened and shut
many times since he left,
taking his bag down the steps
to another house that might have been yours.

Acknowledgments

Along the Alaska Highway
 Northern Review
 Along the Alaska Highway (chapbook)

From the East: First Light, Gastineau Channel
 Alaska Quarterly Review
 Along the Alaska Highway (chapbook)

In the Compass of Unrest
 In the Compass of Unrest (chapbook)

#34, Songs of the Pine-Wife
 Songs of the Pine-Wife (chapbook)

Juneau Fairy Tale
 Permafrost
 In the Compass of Unrest (chapbook)
 The Alaska Reader: Voices from the North

Palm Sunday: Friends Church, Kotzebue
 Sing, Heavenly Muse

The Village Teacher
 Ripples

Wild Swans at Mid-Winter
 Eleven
 Top of the World

The News from Nikolai
 Bits
 In the Dreamlight: Twenty-one Alaskan Writers

Notes from the Umiak-Maker, Kamchatka
 Cirque

A Woman Speaks: Western Alaska
 Wind

The Muskrat Hunter Remembers
 Calapooya Collage

Notes from a Last Summer
 Hawaii Pacific Review

The Priest Visits Toksook Bay
 To the Waters and the Wild (chapbook)

On the Alaska Ferry, along the British Columbia Coast
 Calapooya Collage

Early Morning, Late August
 Inroads: 27 Alaska Fellowship Writers

Promise, in September
 Inroads: 27 Alaska Fellowship Writers

Kodiak Widow
 Orca
 In the Compass of Unrest (chapbook)
 Only Morning in Her Shoes
 Literature: Reading, Reacting, Writing
 Pushcart Prize #10

Kooshdaka Visits My Daughter
 Alaska Quarterly Review

Skagway: The House on Main Street
Finding the Boundaries

Lynette's Story
In an August Garden (chapbook)

Skunk Cabbage Visits Southeast Alaska
The Strange Fruit

When Spring Came and the Blue Bear Came to Town
Quaint Canoe
The Sky's Own Limit
Grrrrr: A Collection of Poems about Bears

Iris
Permafrost
In an August Garden (chapbook)

Visitors
Flukes
In an August Garden (chapbook)

Thimbleberry
Slant
In an August Garden (chapbook)

School Desk as Garden: Tenakee Springs
Prairie Schooner

Tenakee Springs Garden: January
Prairie Schooner
Walking Ink

The Foxglove Gone Feral: Calhoun Ave.
The Strange Fruit

In the Stone Nursery
Prairie Schooner

Evensong
Willow Springs
In an August Garden (chapbook)

Trees
Common Sense
Northwest Poet's and Artist's Calendar

The Dolly Varden Char: Its Name, Its Dance, Its Prize
Northern Review

In an August Garden, along the Path in Tenakee Springs
Alaska Quarterly Review
In an August Garden (chapbook)

The Abandoned Russian Orthodox Church, Aleknagik: September
The Glens Falls Review

Song of the Soapstone Carver
To the Waters and the Wild (chapbook)
Pushcart Prize #1

Illumination
Crab Creek Review
In an August Garden (chapbook)

Pelican of the Wilderness
Greenfield Review

Choosing Pansies
In an August Garden (chapbook)

Neighbor
> *Permafrost*
> *Dan River Anthology*
> *Hunger and Dreams: The Alaska Women's Anthology*
> *Only Morning in Her Shoes*
> *Waiting for the News of Death*
> *In an August Garden* (chapbook)

Wishkita: House of the Shark
> *Sing, Heavenly Muse*

On Reading a Recipe for Pickled Venison Heart
> *Earth's Daughters #54*

White Lilacs
> *Hunger and Dreams: The Alaska Women's Anthology*
> *Waiting for the News of Death* (chapbook)

In the Raspberry Villages: September
> *Parting Gifts*
> *Poems for the Wild Earth*
> *In an August Garden* (chapbook)

Summer Ends in the High Latitudes
> *Cirque*

Traveling Highway 16, British Columbia
> *Thrush*

Russ, in the Dark Garden
> *Cirque*

The Eagle's Nest
> *Spillway*

After Euthanasia
Thrush

Detour: Driving North on I-5
Through a Distant Lens: Travel Poems

Summer, by Bicycle
Off the Coast

Traveling East, from the Oregon Coast
Dog River Review

In the Gardens at Padden Creek
Naugatuck River Review

Sailing in the San Juan Islands: Late August
Cirque

In a University Town: September
Sue C. Boynton Contest

December Dusk: The Stables off Smith Road
Sue C. Boynton Contest

Tapping the Sugar Maple Trees
These Fragile Lilacs

At Virginia Mason Hospital
Comstock Review

June: On the West Flank of Mt. Baker
Windfall

Transplanting the Poppies
Through a Distant Lens: Travel Poems

At Summer's End
    Heart of the Flower
    Top of the World
    In an August Garden (chapbook)
    Family Circle Easy Gardening

During the Moon of Falling Leaves
    Whatcom Writes!

September: Collecting the Plums
    Thrush

At Hannah's Wedding
    Thrush

The Gardener, in October
    Ibbetson Street #27

Charlie and his Water Lily
    Off the Coast

The Almost Abandoned House: Old Route 213
    The Aurorean

The Walkers, Ulster County
    The Aurorean

Winter on the Banks of the Delaware and Hudson Canal
    CircleShow

Late Winter in High Falls: Waiting for the School Bus
    Pacific Review

The Lost Gospel of the Cooper's Hawk
    The Door Is a Jar

In the Kitchen
The Unaurorean

Tortellini Arrives at the Front Steps
Hawaii Pacific Review

With Splendora, My Friend, among the Tomatoes
Noisy Water: Poetry from Whatcom County, Washington

On Approaching a Fiftieth Wedding Anniversary
Cirque

On the Origin of Stories
The Glens Falls Review
Northwest Poet's and Artist's Calendar

About the Author

I was born in New York in 1942 and brought up in a Revolutionary period house on Long Island. I graduated from the Chapin School in New York and Bryn Mawr College and hold a Ph. D. in Creative Writing from Union Institute and University. After living in Boulder, Colorado, from 1964-1971, I moved with my family to Juneau, Alaska, where I lived from 1971-1998. There I served as Poet Laureate and as Writer-in Residence to the Alaska State Library while also teaching in the Artists-in-the-Schools program and in University within Walls, a statewide prison education program. I served, too, for seven years as head of the Communications Section of the Alaska Department of Fish and Game. After raising three children in Juneau, my husband Martin and I moved to Bellingham, Washington.

Travels through Alaska have informed and inspired my work, which focuses to a large extent on the natural world and our mysterious connections with it. Teaching in prisons and other under-served communities expanded my appreciation for the personal story and the power inherent in telling it. Editing the state's conservation magazine, *Alaska's Wildlife*, taught me discipline in factual writing and responsibility for accuracy. Access to the archives of the Alaska State Library introduced me to the subject of 19th century arctic exploration and its extraordinary adventures. Intrigued, I set out to retrieve what I could of this history and retell some of its chapters before they were lost to oblivion. This fascination led to years of research and three nonfiction books, the last focusing on the 19th century sledge dogs which enabled American explorers to reach the North Pole.

Is it hard for a poet to write prose? Emily Dickinson claimed that poetry is "a fairer house than prose." That might be;

but for me, the two forms complement one another—the economy of poetry and the expansive nature of prose—each pushing against its limits to find balance in the piece. The tension that results gives life and energy to the work.

The inchoate poem is there, waiting inside something you have experienced—a flower, a stone, a comment overheard—and calls you to it. Gradually it becomes more insistent. It wants to be born, but how do you give it the words it needs to take meaningful shape? You look and listen from every possible angle, protecting it as you let it experiment with different voices and images. Time passes. It plays and struggles with various manifestations, calling on you at all hours. You will know when it has found its ultimate shape and voice. Whatever it is—and you might be surprised—it satisfies a hunger you have felt deep within. You will know that in claiming form this creation has enlarged the world and your view of it. Poetry, like the universe, is ever expanding, carrying us into unknown spaces. If poetry is a house, then poetry is what is necessary to build a city.

www.ingramcontent.com/pod-product-compliance
Lightning Source LLC
Chambersburg PA
CBHW021443080526
44588CB00009B/657